52 *Amazingly* SIMPLE SECRETS *for* BETTER GOLF

RICK GRAVES
PGA Golf Professional

Paintings by WILLIAM MANGUM

HARVEST HOUSE PUBLISHERS
EUGENE, OREGON

Acknowledgments

Special thanks to my wife Moonie, who encouraged me to keep writing; to my son Tim, my talented copy editor and an accomplished writer himself; to Terry Glaspey, my editor at Harvest House, without whom this book would not be; but first to God, who gave me any talent in golf I might have.

—Rick

52 Amazingly Simple Secrets for Better Golf

Published by Harvest House Publishers
Eugene, Oregon 97402

ISBN-13: 978-0-7369-1635-6
ISBN-10: 0-7369-1635-0

Design and production by Garborg Design Works, Minneapolis, Minnesota

Printed in China

06 07 08 09 10 11 12 13 / LP / 10 9 8 7 6 5 4 3 2 1

Foreword

Writing four books about the game of golf has provided me the opportunity to work with people such as Jack Nicklaus, the finest player who ever played the game, and Pete Dye, the renowned golf course architect. In the process, I have also had the blessing to meet such fabled golfers as Arnold Palmer, Gary Player, Lee Trevino, Johnny Miller, and Tom Watson. Watching them compete and hearing their stories taught me that the key to the game is concentrating on the basics rather than relying on the fancy complex methods that are so common among golf instructors these days.

Observing these great players helped me realize an important truth that has greatly improved my own game: Keep it simple! Whether it is Nicklaus, Palmer, Tiger Woods, or Phil Mickelson—they know how to concentrate on one or two key things as they tee it up for a competitive round.

My friend Rick Graves, a seasoned PGA professional, captures the essence of this method so well in *52 Amazingly Simple Secrets for Better Golf*. His easy-to-remember thoughts are guaranteed to lower your score and make you the envy of your golf friends. So read on, take notes, and then let Rick's tips be a part of your preparation for every round you play.

Mark Shaw
Author of *Jack Nicklaus: Golf's Greatest Champion; Bury Me in a Pot Bunker; Diamonds in the Rough;* and *From Birdies to Bunkers*

Golf is a great game because it allows one to run the gamut of emotions in a four-hour span without harming anyone.

BOB JONES

Simple, But Powerful

$E=mc^2$.

It's a simple equation, but it represents one of our greatest breakthroughs—Einstein's theory of relativity. Einstein's genius was such that he could reduce chalkboards full of equations into this one elegant end result.

Sometimes simple can be better. We tend to make things so complex. Anyone who has spent time studying the mountains of golf instruction books knows it is easy to be overwhelmed and confused by all the suggestions they offer and advice they give. Perhaps you've been left feeling like you'll never be able to remember all this complicated teaching! Or you stand over a putt and your mind is overrun with dozens of thoughts about stance, grip, pace, and other factors in making a good stroke. Hard to make a good run at it with all that going on in your head!

Well, there's hope! I'm no Einstein, but I've spent nearly fifty years teaching, playing, and studying the game, and I've been able to condense my thinking into 52 amazingly simple truths about golf. They include psychological, technical, and practice tips on the full swing,

chipping,
pitching,
sand play,
and putting,
as well as
course
management
and the vitally
important mental
side of the game.
These simple
thoughts, if taken
to heart, can teach
you how to approach
the game with more
confidence and greater
results than you ever imagined.

So read and re-read this book. You might consider focusing on one tip each week for a year. Put this book in your golf bag, practice often, and make all of these tips a part of your game. If you do, 52 weeks from today you may be looking at a scorecard with a number lower than you ever thought possible! Nothing would make me happier.

God bless,
Rick Graves
PGA Professional

#1

For any golfer, the first shot often foreshadows the entire day. An exceptionally good first drive may inspire you to new heights, and an embarrassing one may undermine your confidence.

Prepare for that crucial first swing. Before teeing off, stretch, hit practice balls, and *visualize a perfect shot.*

For every shot you hit on the practice range, hit *three* around the practice green.

Ninety percent of your ability to score depends on your performance from 30 yards in.

A half-hour before you tee off, do everything in slow motion. Walk slowly; talk slowly; put your glove on slowly; breathe slowly; practice-swing very slowly; remove your headcover slowly. Then—your swing tempo for the day just might be slow.

#4

To ensure correct positioning of the club at the top of your backswing, execute a swing and freeze at the top.

Remove your left hand from the grip, holding it loosely with only your right hand. The club will drop. If the shaft lands between your neck and right shoulder, your swing plane is correct.

The club should be gripped in the *fingers* of your right hand. Make certain the lifeline of your right hand suffocates your left thumb, which should be straight down the top of the shaft.

"Don't touch it, Lord. It'll cost him two strokes."

LEE TREVINO,
after a pro-am partner skied his tee shot

#6

Metaphorically, play golf on shock absorbers—*not* stilts.

Make sure your legs are well-flexed, with your left knee pointing in toward the ball on the backswing. Kick your right knee toward the ball on the forward swing.

#7

Swing shoulder-to-shoulder.

Have your left shoulder under your chin at the top of your backswing. Feel your right shoulder under your chin as the clubhead is three feet past impact.

#8

***See* the ball being struck by the clubhead.**

When striking a teed ball, keep your head in position long enough to see the tee after impact; then, let your body-turn bring your head around to view the ball's flight.

When aligning, aim your feet slightly to the left.

Every player's tendency is to address the ball with their feet aiming to the right of the intended target line. This common error usually causes an incomplete shoulder turn as the player attempts to *pull* the shot back to the target.

Promise yourself on the first tee that you will give *every* shot your full attention.

If you miss a shot, dismiss it as your best effort—*no* regrets. Approach the next shot mentally in the present. If your thoughts are focused 100 percent on the shot at hand, you will have no room in your mind to think about previous errors.

I want to live to 112 so I can shoot my age.

AUTHOR UNKNOWN

william mangum

#11

Swing your driver with the intent of sweeping the ball *up,* leaving the tee intact.

The driver is the only club in the bag that requires an additional piece of equipment (the tee). Because of the driver's low loft, one must make an extra effort to hit up on the ball.

#12

The first move of your backswing should be your shirt placket turning away from your target; the first move of your downswing should be your belt buckle turning back toward the hole.

#13

Fear and indecision about a shot usually lead to an incomplete shoulder turn.

Trust your swing.

A bad shot often costs a player a few more strokes. A bad temper often costs a player his whole day.

Whatever happens, try to remain calm.

If a particular hole intimidates you from the tee, pretend you are on the tee of a favorite similar hole and make *that* swing.

Golf course architects are paid big money to design golf puzzles. Solve the puzzle on each hole before teeing off.

Turn your brain off so your body can hit the golf ball without interference.

AUTHOR UNKNOWN

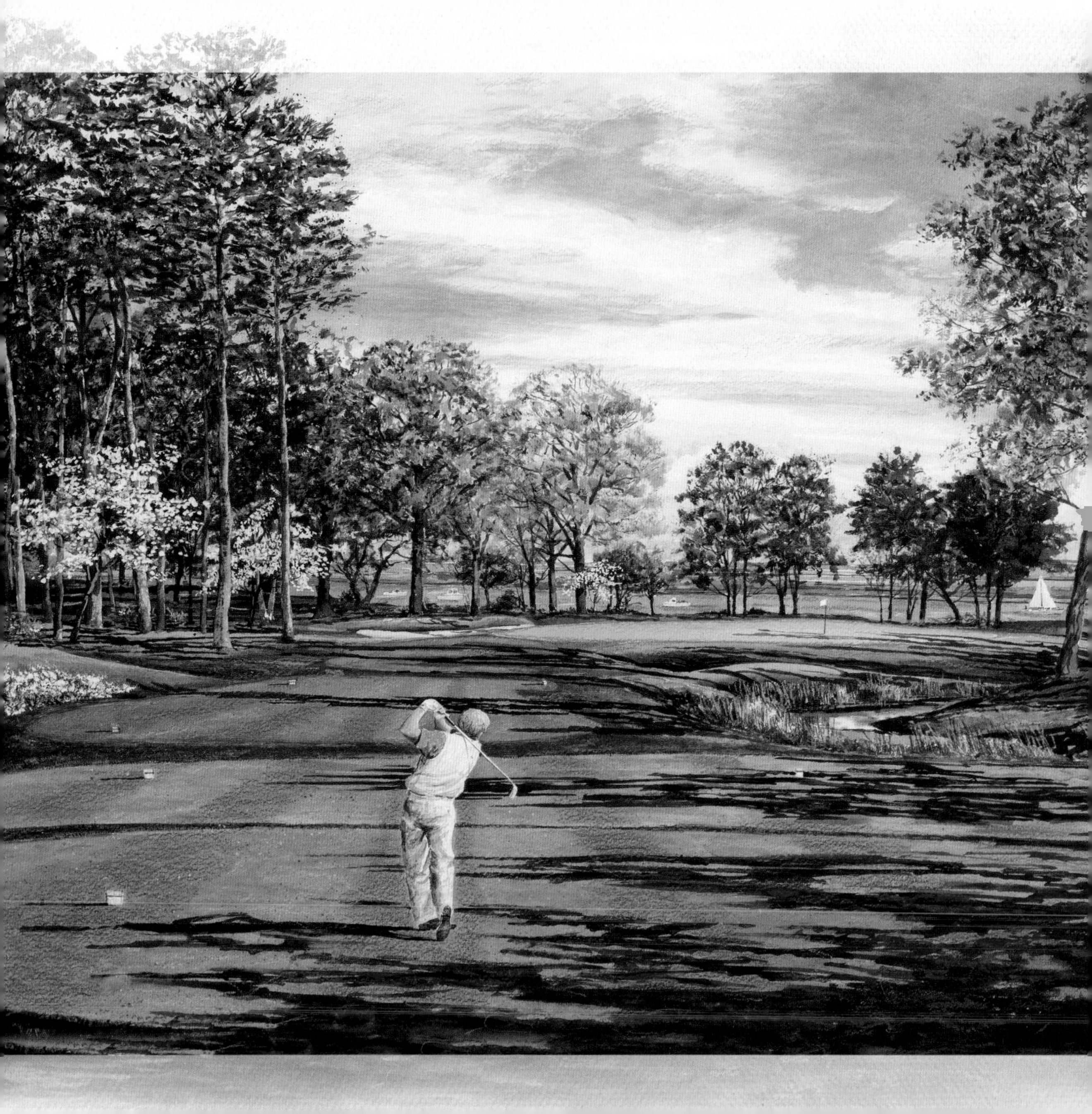

#17

When preparing to play on an extremely windy day, add ten shots to par.

You'll play in a relaxed state of mind, and you'll shoot a lower score than many others.

#18

To learn proper delayed hit (release), grip your driver upside down—with your hands near the clubhead—and swing normally.

Listen for a distinct swish sound created as you swing. Ensure that this noise occurs *at* or *past* where the ball would be on the ground.

#19

Finish your swing completely up on your right toe with your belt buckle toward the target.

Hold your right foot perpendicular to the ground until the ball lands. This method cultivates perfect balance.

My game's improving.
My whiffs are much closer to the ball.

JACK LEMMON

William Mangum

Here's the final word on excuses and bad luck: The ball goes where *you* hit it!

Address the ball against the sweet spot of the club.

If you don't think hitting the ball on the sweet spot is vital, bounce a ball on different spots of the clubface. When you hit the sweet spot, you may have to duck as the ball leaps off the clubface.

Your first putt on the practice green should be under one foot.

This technique starts your day off right. The sound of the ball rattling around in the cup is a powerful association of past success and puts you in a resourceful frame of mind. Lipping out your first few putts of the day can easily start a negative train of thought.

NEHURST
2
THE BLUE CLICK
COLONEL
GOLF BALLS
ST MUNGO MFG. CO OF AMERICA
NEWARK N.J.
New York, Boston, Philadelphia, Atlanta, Chicago, San Francisco
PINEHURST COUNTRY CLUB
Course No. 2
SELF Bill
Bobby

#23

If you are having a spectacular round, stay loose and enjoy it—but realize that the bubble may burst at any time.

By keeping expectations at a reasonable level, you just might get to the clubhouse before the playing streak ends. In any round, "Golf giveth and golf taketh away," so keep smiling no matter what happens to the magic. When the round is over, go to the range and figure out what went *right*. Jot your findings down in a journal and use these insights later.

Try to *never* hit two bad shots in a row. Make it a goal to always follow a bad shot with a good shot. It needn't be a career-best or heroic shot—just a good one.

If you are going to play a shot safe, play it extremely safe. When you take a gamble, the reward should far outweigh the risk.

A bogey is easier to take mentally and recover from than a triple bogey, which can demoralize you completely.

Once a month, play nine holes with only a three iron, seven iron, sand wedge, and putter.

You'll discover new facets of shot-making.

A good exercise at the range is to hit your sand wedge as smoothly as you can.

Try to hit all other clubs in your bag with the same smooth swing—starting with your pitching wedge. If you begin swinging too hard, do not advance to the next club until you regain the desired smoothness. Some days you can maintain the smoothness all the way through the driver, and some days you can't get past the eight iron. But whatever the outcome, you will have practiced good swing tempo.

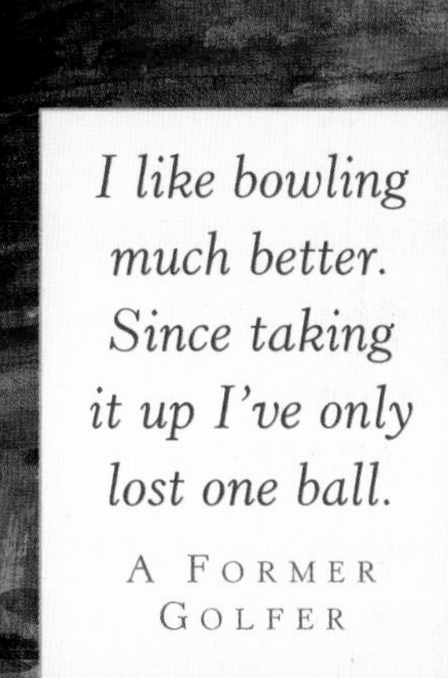

I like bowling much better. Since taking it up I've only lost one ball.

A FORMER GOLFER

Golf is an expensive game. Visit your PGA professional and ask him to help you select the best equipment you can afford, thus maximizing your potential.

A professional of today can muster a good score with ancient Hickory clubs only because he sports an excellent swing. *The less talent you have, the more you need well-fitted equipment.* For example, properly fitted shafts are essential to producing good golf shots. Weak shafts over-oscillate throughout the swing, causing shots to fly both left and right. You will not be able to fix this fault even with practice.

#29

Know whether your tee shots on a given day tend to draw or fade.

If you are fading, aim down the left quarter of the fairway, using the other three-quarters as leeway; likewise, if you are drawing, aim for the right quarter of the fairway. Players who aim for the center of a fairway or directly at a flagstick have less room for error.

Choose your club for pitching and chipping relative to how much running-room there is to the hole.

The less running-room, the more loft is needed on the clubface. A highly-lofted shot lands softer and stops quicker than a lowly-lofted one; however, the less-lofted club lands with less backspin and is a more predictable shot. Select the club with the lowest loft that carries the ball safely onto the green and stops the ball near the hole.

Hit *down* on chips and pitches.

Trying to swing up on these shots—in an attempt to lift the ball up—is self-defeating. By hitting down on chips and pitches, you are assuring that the leading edge of the clubface will slide under the ball without skulling it (smacking the middle or top of the ball).

A sand wedge is not just for sand play.

To play a sand wedge from around the green, follow this formula:

1. Choke the club to the end of the grip.
2. Play the ball off your back foot.
3. Grip the club very firmly and strike the ball with an authoritative "pop."
4. Prevent your left wrist from hinging on the follow-through.
5. Leave your head in position. *Listen* for the ball to hit the green before you look to see the results.

In a bunker, dig your feet about an inch into the sand.

There are two reasons for this: 1) your feet will be stable during your swing, enabling your club to consistently strike the same spot in the sand; and 2) the arc of your swing will travel through the sand about one inch *under* the ball, causing an effective explosion shot.

#34

On sand shots, don't adjust your swing in order to hit behind the ball; instead, put the ball an inch or two forward in your stance.

#35

When your ball is buried in a greenside bunker, shut the sand wedge's face 30 degrees.

Maintain a firm left-hand grip and strike one inch behind the ball with the hooded clubface. Because the clubface's toe is knifing *into* the sand—without the club's flange bouncing *off* the sand—the wedge continues downward, and the ball is jettisoned up and out with no backspin. A little experimentation using this technique will arm you with a valuable new shot.

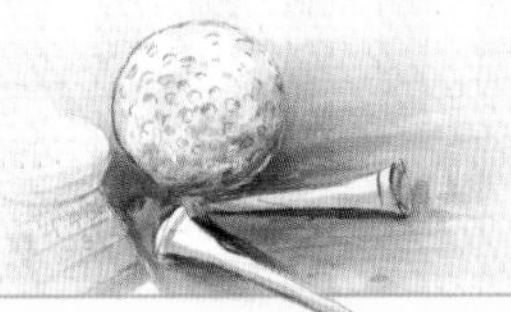

Don't be too proud to take lessons. I'm not.

JACK NICKLAUS

Imagine bunker shots as an attempt to shower the green with sand.

Pretend that your ball is just another grain among the sand. With that metaphor in mind, you'll be surprised how effortlessly your ball comes out.

To hit a bunker shot 30 feet, swing as hard as you would to hit a fairway shot 30 yards.

Many golfers under-swing on bunker shots because the brain resists swinging hard for a short shot. Overcome this tendency by forcing yourself to explode through the shot.

When hitting out of fairway bunkers, minimize your hip-turn on the backswing.

The more I practice, the luckier I get.

BEN HOGAN

#39

When playing side hill lies, expect your ball's flight to follow the same direction that the ball would roll down the hill. A ball above your feet is likely to be pulled, and one below your feet is likely to be pushed.

#40

On uphill and downhill lies, let your left shoulder "follow the hill."

In other words, on a downhill lie, your left shoulder should be low; on an uphill lie, your left shoulder should be high.

Never rush a short putt.

Mark your ball and gather yourself before attempting any putt.

On short putts, *listen*—don't look—for the ball to go in.

PUTTER BOY
1912

Pick a line for a putt and believe in it.

Vividly *visualize* that line. You'll make a better stroke and more putts.

On putts, address the ball just inside your left foot.

Playing the ball too far back in your stance causes you to hit down on it. The ball will bounce all the way to the hole—and probably rim out of the cup.

***Always* accelerate through a putt.**

A folding left wrist on the forward stroke of a short putt is a prescription for failure. Keep the putter-head even with or behind your hands on short putts.

Triangulate on breaking putts.

On the side of the break, stand across from your ball. Step back until your ball, you, and the cup form the corners of an equilateral triangle. Once you reach this position, scrutinize the steepness of the hill. You will gain an overall perspective of the slope and distance of the putt.

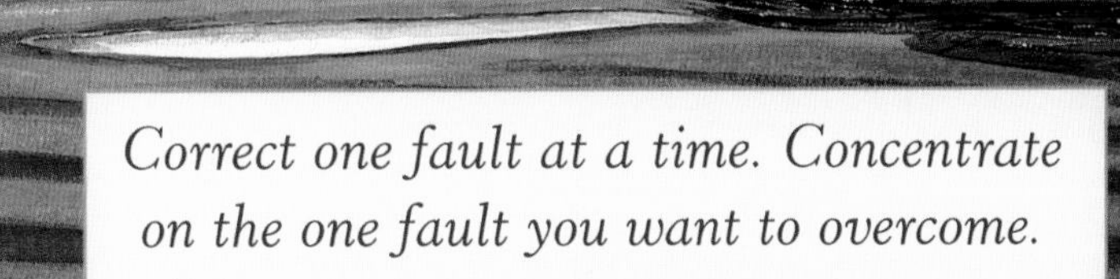

Correct one fault at a time. Concentrate on the one fault you want to overcome.

SAM SNEAD

The putting expression "Never up, never in" is misleading.

A ball lingering at the edge of a cup is more likely to drop in than is one struck hard enough to run three feet by the hole. Leave yourself more tap-ins than three-footers.

Buy a high-quality, correctly-fitted putter and *marry* it!

A player who frequently changes his putter is unable to cultivate a friendship with it. Bobby Jones had Calamity Jane; Ben Crenshaw uses Little Ben. Gary Player has carried the same beat-up black putter for years, and Jack Nicklaus logged most of his wins with his George Low model. A cumulative degree of effectiveness seems to be gained by sticking with the same putter for years on end.

Learn the unplayable lie rule and lateral water hazard rule well. They will become your good friends.

Interestingly, if you apply these rules properly, those who are unfamiliar with the *Rules of Golf* may accuse you of cheating!

Golf is a game for ladies and gentlemen.

You are your own judge and jury. Take as much pride in calling a tough ruling on yourself as you would in sinking a long putt. The golf course is one of the few places where a person's true character reveals itself for others to observe. Be impeccable!

> *Success in golf depends less on strength of body than upon strength of mind and character.*
>
> ARNOLD PALMER

People who cannot afford to play golf are probably faced with more challenges than those who can.

So let us all try to count our blessings—as well as our strokes—on the golf course. And remember—*it's just a game!*